LITTLE **TOPIC BOOK** OF

Where We Live

Published 2010 by A&C Black Publishers Limited
36 Soho Square, London W1D 3QY
www.acblack.com

ISBN 978-1-9060-2966-1

Text © Liz Powlay 2010
Design © Lynda Murray
Photographs © Fotolia
Cover photo © Fotolia

A CIP record for this publication is available from the British Library.

Printed in Great Britain by Latimer Trend & Company Limited

This book is produced using paper that is made from wood grown
in managed, sustainable forests. It is natural, renewable and
recyclable. The logging and manufacturing processes conform to
the environmental regulations of the country of origin.

To see our full range of titles
visit **www.acblack.com**

Contents

Introduction

Planning ideas

Well-planned activities in a stimulating learning environment are the key to making children's learning relevant, exciting and effective. Planning should involve all practitioners in a setting working together, sharing ideas and using their combined knowledge of the children to provide appropriate learning experiences.

The Early Years Foundation Stage includes six areas of Learning and Development that cover all aspects of the curriculum. All settings need to plan their learning environments carefully to include opportunities for children to develop in each area.

Many early years settings choose to plan around a 'topic' or theme so that the activities are integrated and cross-curricular. This creates connections in children's thinking as they play and results in more meaningful learning. This series of topic books provides a comprehensive collection of ideas and activities for practitioners to 'dip and pick' from when planning.

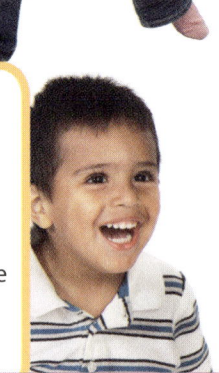

Looking and listening

Ongoing assessment of children is an essential part of early years planning. Looking, listening and noting down daily observations will help inform future planning so it can be appropriate to children's needs and absorbing and relevant to children's interests.

How to use this book

The book is divided into sections covering ten themes relating to the topic 'Where We Live', such as Inside our homes and Animal homes. Each section contains a set of exciting activities to dip into and select from. Each activity includes links to the relevant Early Learning Goals. The Goals are numbered in the order in which they appear in the Statutory Framework for the EYFS, so, for example, PSED 1 is 'Continue to be interested, excited and motivated to learn'.

Coat hanger houses

ELGs: PSED 2, 5; CLL 6, 8; KUW 9, CD 2

What you need

- large plain paper bags or make some from large sheets of paper
- coat hangers
- washing line
- marker pens
- coloured paper
- collage materials
- scissors
- glue.

What you do

- Talk to the children about what their home looks like and what they like about it.

- Invite them to make a picture of their home on the paper bag, using the paper, pens and collage materials.

- Place the coat hanger in the bag at the top, leaving the hook free.

- Glue the bag along the open edge to seal.

- When dry hang up on the washing line to make a street of houses.

And another idea

Place pictures from magazines or photographs of rooms on the other side of the bag to show what rooms are inside the house.

My little house

ELGs: CLL 4; KUW 6

What you need

- copy of the rhyme 'My Little House' (see page 70)
- paper
- scissors
- glue
- wooden lolly sticks
- string
- sticky tape.

What you do

- Share the rhyme together and talk about some of the differences between old and new houses.

- Invite the children to make an old bendy house by cutting off the two top corners from a square of paper and adding a triangle for the roof.

- Add windows and doors with smaller pieces of paper.

- Make a fold across the house near the centre.

- On the back of the house, secure a lolly stick to the bottom part of the house and fasten string to the top part.

- Say the rhyme again, holding the house by the stick to move it from side to side and using the string to make the house bend up and down.

And another idea

Take recycled materials such as boxes, paper cups, clean plastic pots and tins and make model houses that will fall down when a breeze blows, using a hair dryer or fan on cold.

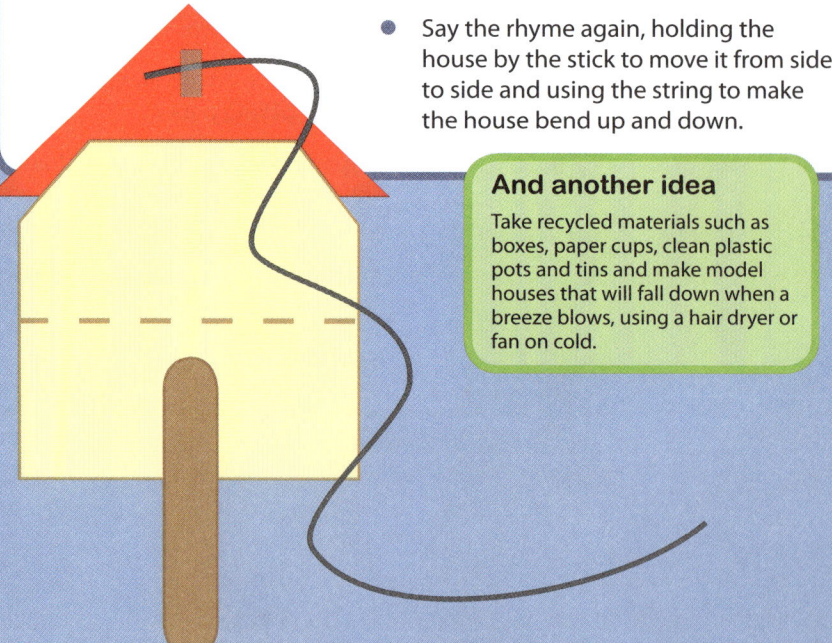

Gingerbread houses

ELGs: PSED 8, CLL 14, 15, 18; PSRN 2, 3, 9, 11; PD 7

What you need

- recipe and ingredients for gingerbread (see page 76)
- bowl, spoon, rolling pin, table knives, small shape cutters
- oven, pieces of baking paper, baking sheet
- pencils.

What you do

- Check for any allergies or dietary requirements and adapt the recipe if necessary.

- Explain to the children that they are going to make gingerbread houses.

- Read through the recipe together.

- Weigh out the ingredients and make the dough, taking turns to weigh and mix.

- Share out the dough and roll out on a piece of baking paper.

- Help the children cut out the shape of a house with a knife and cut out windows with the cutters. Name the shapes used.

- Ask the children to write their names on their baking paper.

- Bake the houses and leave to cool.

Photo-fit houses

ELGs: PSED 9, 10; CLL 5; PSRN 11, 12;
KUW 3, 7, 9, 10; CD 1, 2

What you need

- camera
- local area with a variety of homes
- paper
- glue
- scissors.

What you do

- Before going out, talk to the children about how they need to behave to stay safe.

- Go for a walk and look at and talk about all the different features on the homes – doors, windows, chimneys, roofs.

- Help the children to take photographs of these.

- Print off, enlarging if necessary.

- Invite the children to use the photographs to design their dream house.

- Glue the finished designs on to paper.

- Display these or use them in the role-play estate agents.

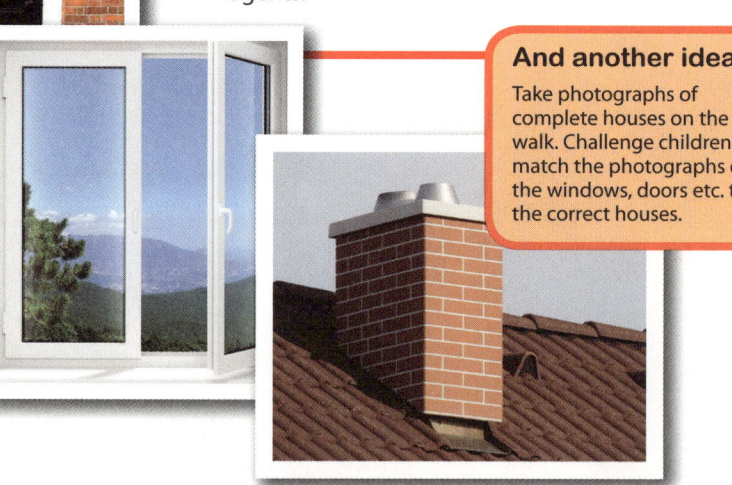

And another idea

Take photographs of complete houses on the walk. Challenge children to match the photographs of the windows, doors etc. to the correct houses.

Origami houses

ELGs: PSED 3, 6; CLL 3; KUW 11; PD 8; CD 3

What you need

- video clips or photographs of origami
- squares of thin paper, no smaller than 15cms
- mark making materials
- pre-made origami house (see instructions on page 77)
- wire and thread to make a mobile

What you do

- Explain that origami is the art of folding paper to make objects. The word origami comes from Japan, but it is a skill found all over Asia.

- Show the children the photographs or video clips.

- Show the children the pre-made house and then demonstrate how to make one. Emphasise the need to concentrate on what you are doing.

- Help the children fold the paper to make a house, taking care to fold as accurately as possible.

- Decorate it with the pens.

- Hang up as a mobile so the houses move in the breeze.

And another idea

By using rectangles of paper and only folding one side it is possible to make different sized and shaped houses. Glue the houses on to small boxes and use to make villages, towns and cities.

Sand clay houses

ELGs: PSED 2; PSRN 1, 3

Sand clay recipe
(makes 3 models)

What you need:
- 2 mugs sand
- 3 mugs cornflour
- 1 mug PVA glue
- 1 mug water
- 1 mug plain flour

What to do:
Mix together all the ingredients to form a clay-like dough.

What you need
- bowl, spoon, mug
- ingredients for sand clay
- modelling tools
- pictures and photographs of children's houses.

What you do

- Look at the pictures and photographs. Talk about the size, shape and features of the children's houses.

- Invite the children to make a model of their house.

- Help the children measure out the materials and make the sand clay dough.

- Using the pictures as a guide help the children make a model of their house or a relative's house if they live in a flat. Start with a block of dough in the shape of their house and then use the tools to make the windows, doors and roof tiles.

- Leave to dry and paint.

And another idea
Make flat models and when dry glue on to card to give as a gift to the child's family.

Igloos

ELGs: PSED 6, 12, 13; CLL 3, 5, PSRN 11;
KUW 5, 9, 11; PD 8, CD 3

What you need

- white modelling materials:
  - sugar cubes
  - soapflake mud
  - ice cubes
  - construction bricks
  - marshmallows
- paper bowls
- photographs of igloos
- toy polar bear.

Soapflake mud

What you need:
- 1 roll white toilet tissue
- 1 cup soap flakes
- warm water.

What to do:
Tear the toilet tissue into small pieces. Mix together the tissue and soap in a bowl. Add water slowly, mixing and squeezing the mixture using hands until a thick 'mud' is made that can be moulded into blocks.

What you do

- Explain to the children how an igloo is the traditional winter hunting home of the Inuit people. An igloo is not a permanent home, as it is built of snow and ice so it melts in warmer weather, but it provides a strong, safe place to live in the winter. It is so hard and strong that a polar bear can climb on top of an igloo without it collapsing!

- Look at the shape of an igloo and how it is made of blocks.

- Using an upside-down bowl as a base, invite the children to select a modelling material (or use the soapflake mud) and try to make an igloo that will be strong enough for a polar bear to stand on.

- Discuss with the children their choice of material and whether it was successful or not.

- Encourage them to try with another material if theirs is not working well.

And another idea
Make a role play igloo with large cardboard boxes painted white and glued together.

Homes bingo

ELGs: PSED 3, 8, 13; CLL 3, 5, 9; KUW 3, 9, 11

What you need

- small pictures of around 12 different types of homes from around the world (several copies of each picture)
- card
- small bag or box
- counters.

What you do

- Make bingo boards using six different pictures on each board. Write the name of each home under the picture.

- Place a copy of each picture used, in the bag or box.

- Talk about the pictures, looking at how each home is made and how they all differ. Explain that this can be due to the weather, if the people move around a lot and what materials they have locally to build with.

- Explain to the children that if a picture featured on their board comes out of the bag they can place a counter on it.

- Pull out each picture, saying the sounds in the name of the home in the order they occur, before saying the complete word and describing how the home is made.

- The winner is the first child to cover their pictures, or play until all pictures are covered.

And another idea

Play a pairs game online at www.sadlier-oxford.com/readers/socialstudies/book2/game.htm finding matching pictures of houses from around the world.

Where in the world books

ELGs: CLL 18, 19; KUW 9, 10

What you do

- Talk about where the children live, helping them to appreciate that they live in a street that is usually part of a village, town or city and that this is in a specific area within the country and the world.

- Look at the pictures of the area and show the children where this is on the country map and the world.

- Ask the children to take photographs of each other and print them off.

- Help the children to make books to show where they are in the world, placing their photograph on the first page. On subsequent pages, place a drawing, photographs or maps to show their room, house, street, immediate area, locality, country and finally the world. Mark on the maps where they live.

- Invite the child to write their name on the front cover and to decorate it with pictures of things they like in the environment around them.

What you need

- plain paper made into a book with eight pages for each child
- digital camera and printer
- pictures and maps of immediate and local area
- pictures and maps showing the shape of the country.

And another idea

Make books showing where in the world children from other countries live and the type of places they live in.

Build a house

ELGs: PSED 1, 2, 7, 8, 12; CLL 1, 8, 8, 11, 17, 18, 19;
KUW 1, 5, 6; PD 1, 2, 7, 8

What you need

- photographs of homes around the world
- construction materials, large and small scale
- large sheets of fabric and cardboard
- wood
- clothes pegs, bulldog clips, string

What you do

- Look at the photographs of the houses together.

- Invite small groups of children to choose the one they would like to try to make.

- Discuss how the construction materials, fabric, card and wood could be used to make a house and how they could be fastened together using the pegs, clips and string.

- Ask the children to decide which ones would be most suitable to build a model of their house.

- Invite the children to work together to make the house on either a large or small scale.

- Support them as they work together, ensuring they work safely with larger items.

- Take photographs of the construction process and finished product. Display the photographs alongside the original picture.

- Help the children to write captions for the photographs describing the building process.

And another idea

Make small models of the houses and display them on a map of the world.

International doll's house

ELGs: PSED 13; KUW 5, 6; PD 8; CD 1, 2, 3

What you need
- shoe box for each child
- photographs of different rooms inside homes around the world
- craft resources.

What you do

- Explain to the children that the insides of homes vary from country to country and home to home.

- Look at the differences using the photographs.

- Invite the children to turn a shoe box into a room of their choice using the materials.

- Join the finished rooms together to form a series of houses.

And another idea
Make small figures by laminating pictures of people from around the world to use in the houses for small world play.

Festival home

ELGs: PSED 5, 6, 13; CLL 16; KUW 11; CD 4, 5

What you need

- role-play area
- information on a festival
- resources linked to the festival.

What you do

- Explain to the children how people decorate their homes for festivals. Refer to festivals that the children have celebrated such as Christmas or Divali.

- Choose a festival to celebrate with the children, linked to an interest or child in the group. For example Hinamatursi Day which is 'The day of the Dolls' when Japanese families commemorate their ancestors. Talk about the festival and what the children might be able to bring in, such as a toy or doll.

- With the children, set up the role-play area. Include, for example, a story or book about Japanese life, resources to have a Japanese tea party, materials to make a Japanese style home (decorated for a festival), pictures of children celebrating Hinamatursi Day, resources to make kimonos from paper or fabric, appropriate music and so on.

- Celebrate the festival, reading the books, trying food, making kimonos and listening to and dancing to the music.

- Wear the kimonos to have a real or pretend tea party.

And another idea

For festival ideas refer to a book such as *Children Just Like Me: A Unique Celebration of Children Around the World* by Anabel Kindersley (Dorling Kindersley)

Home helper

ELGs: PSED 4, 5, 7, 9, 10; CLL 3, 6, 8, 11, 17, 18, 19; KUW 8

What you need

- large piece of paper
- 'Clean and tidy' box containing items from a kitchen, bathroom, living room and bedroom such as washing-up liquid, plates, clothes, toys, duster
- pens.

What you do

- Explain to the children that it takes a lot of work to keep a home clean and tidy.

- Ask them who helps at home and who does most of the cleaning and tidying. Talk about why it is important to help and share the work.

- Invite the children to take turns to choose an item from the box and think why it might be in there or how they could use it to help.

- Think about how the children can help in different rooms of the house. Draw a large outline shape of a house showing four empty rooms: kitchen, bathroom, living room and bedroom. Help the children to record their suggestions through writing and drawing on the house picture.

And another idea

Make up a 'Clean and tidy' song together to the tune of 'Here we go Round the Mulberry Bush', such as 'This is the way we wash the pots' or 'This is the way we pick up our toys'.

Alphabet hunt

ELGs: PSED 2; CLL 10, 14, 18, 19

What you need

- alphabet books
- pictures of different rooms in the house
- plain paper book with the letters of the alphabet written one to a page.

What you do

- Show the children the alphabet books and point out how each page shows items beginning with that letter.

- Invite the children to make an alphabet book for things found in the home.

- Using the children's ideas, the pictures or a visit to a house find things for each letter of the alphabet and record them through writing, drawing and photographs.

- Arrange these on the appropriate page.

- Share the finished book together.

And another idea

Use the pictures to play I–spy looking for items beginning with different sounds of the alphabet.

Touchy and feely home

ELGs: PSED 1, 3, 8; CLL 3, 5, 8; KUW 1, 3

What you need

- samples of things from around the house with different textures such as:
  - foil
  - cling film
  - carpets
  - fabrics
  - towelling
  - papers
  - wallpapers
  - cleaning cloths
  - lace
- large box or bag
- scissors, glue
- music.

What you do

- Spread out the samples and sit in a circle around them.

- Help the children name the samples and say where in the house they might be found.

- Handle them and discuss whether they are hard, soft, cold or warm to the touch, flexible, textured, smooth, rough and so on.

- Ask the children to place the samples in the box or bag.

- Play the music and pass the bag around. When the music stops, a child feels a sample in the bag and tries to guess what it is, before pulling it out. Continue until all the samples have been used.

And another idea

Take outline drawings of the front of a house on card, showing roof, windows, door, and walls. Ask the children to select from the sample pieces textures that match the feel of the parts of the house and glue them in place. For example, foil might be used on the windows as it is smooth and cold like glass.

New home tea party

ELGs: PSED 7, 8; CLL 4; PD 2, 7; CD 2

What you need

- large blocks or painted detergent boxes
- role-play cup, saucer and plate for each child
- jug of juice, water or milk and box containing a simple snack
- cup drawn on the floor or made from masking tape.

What you do

- Explain to the children that people often celebrate having a new home by inviting friends over, to come into the house and have a drink.

- Suggest that they have a tea party together, sharing some food and drink.

- Near to the cup on the floor build the 'house' by making a large open rectangle with the bricks or boxes and placing the tea things inside.

- Make a circle, with the adult standing on the cup drawn on the floor, holding hands, then walk round in a circle saying or singing this rhyme:

  We're having a party, a party, a party.
  We're having a party! Who will come to tea?

- The child who is standing on the cup at the end of the rhyme goes into the house and sits down taking a cup, saucer and plate.

- Continue, using the second verse:

  (name of child) is at the party, the party, the party.
  (name of child) is at the party. Who will come to tea?

  adding in the name of the child who went into the house each time, until all the children are inside.

- Help the children share out the snack (such as cheese and crackers or apple slices and raisins) and drinks and enjoy the tea party.

And another idea

Sing some tea themed songs after the tea party such as 'Polly Put the Kettle On' and 'I'm a Little Tea Pot'.

Favourite art

ELGs: PSED 5, 13, 14; CLL 6, 8; PD 8; CD 1, 2, 3

What you need

- favourite pictures from home
- paper
- art materials.

What you do

- Ask the children to bring in their favourite picture from home. This could be a photograph of it, a photocopy or the original. Display the children's pictures and then invite them to show their picture to the others, saying why they like it and where it is in their home.

- Take a photograph of any originals before sending them home.

- Invite the children to make a copy of their picture to display in the setting, using the art materials, copying the detail and colours as carefully as possible.

- Display the pictures with a card alongside saying why the child likes the original picture and add a photograph or copy of the original.

And another idea

Take the children on a visit to an art gallery. To help the children look at the pictures carefully set challenges around two or three pictures – which picture uses the most colours? Which has the smallest leaf?

Bath time babies

ELGs: PSED 5, 11, 12; CLL 6, 7;
KUW 8; PD 5, 7, 8; CD 1, 2, 5

What you need

- bathable dolls
- dolls' bath or baby bath, warm water
- bathtime items such as:
  - bubble bath
  - sponge
  - towels
  - bath toys
- clothes and nappies for the dolls.

What you do

- Talk to the children about how some rooms in the house have a special purpose, often with a routine or special way to do things and how these can help us stay healthy and safe.

- Discuss the bath and bedtime routines that the children have.

- Invite the children to act out the bathtime routines they have with the dolls or make up a new one with a friend.

- At the end of the bathtime play, invite them to dry the dolls and dress them ready for bed.

And another idea

Set up the role-play area with dolls and a bathroom and bedroom in addition to the more frequently found kitchen and sitting areas. Encourage the children to act out the routines and special times they go through at home, with the dolls.

Making a wormery

ELGs: PSED 1, 9, 10; KUW 2, 3

What you need

- large clear plastic container such as an old fish tank
- garden soil or potting compost
- sand
- water
- grass clippings
- dead leaves
- dry rolled oats
- 10 to 12 worms
- very fine net
- newspaper
- string

What you do

- Go on a worm hunt with the children, looking under stones and in the soil or compost.

- Talk about why we rarely see worms in the day (because worms are nocturnal and active at night, when they drag leaves and grass down into the ground to eat).

- Explain to the children that they can make a worm home to see what the worms do.

- Help them to set up the home. Place a 3cm layer of soil into the bottom of the container then add a layer of sand to the same depth. Repeat the layers to within 5cm of the top.

- Pour over a mug of water.

- Place the grass, leaves and oats on top.

- Add the worms and cover in the net and secure. Place the container in a cool area away from sun and heat.

- To make the worms think it's night and become active, wrap the container in newspaper. Place a piece loosely on the top, so air can still reach the tank.

- Regularly remove the paper to observe the worms and their tunnels.

- Invite the children to take responsibility for feeding them and sprinkling with water daily to stop the soil drying out.

- Release the worms in the garden after three or four weeks.

And another idea
Make an ant farm in the same way, feeding them fruit, vegetables, bread or cake crumbs.

Beehive moves

ELGs: CLL 16, 19; PSRN 10; KUW 2; PD 1, 2, 4, 7; CD 1, 4, 5

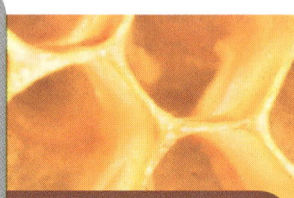

What you need

- photographs of bees
- lengths of yellow card and ribbon about 4 cm wide
- black paint or marker pens
- black pipe cleaners
- stapler
- short canes
- 'Flight of the Bumblebee' music by Rimsky-Korsakov
- large area outside or in with a 'beehive' with a sheet or fabric decorated to resemble a hive, draped over a child's dome tent.

What you do

● Look at the pattern of stripes on the bee's body in the photographs. Talk about how some bees live in hives, some in holes in the ground and how they communicate to each other about where there is food through movements like a dance.

● Invite the children to make a bee headband by drawing and painting black stripes on the card then adding pipe cleaner antennae. Make into a band that fits the child's head and secure with staples.

● Draw black stripes on the ribbon and tie two or three lengths of ribbon on to the canes, at the top.

● Listen to the music, then invite the children to move in lines and circles 'drawing' in the air with the ribbons as they move towards the 'hive'.

● Take turns to be the bees in the hive and the bees dancing to show where there is food.

And another idea

Decorate paper plates to resemble bees by painting on black and yellow stripes. Make wings from black tissue-paper decorated with spiral and circle shapes, drawn on with a silver pen. Hang up to 'dance' in the breeze.

Spiders' webs

ELGs: PSED 3, 8; CLL 16; PSRN 1, 3, 4, 11; KUW 2; PD 2

What you need

- black cardboard circles
- book about spiders with photographs of spiders' webs
- dice
- hole punch
- silver pen
- thin silver ribbon or silver cord.

What you do

- Make six holes at regular intervals around the edge of the circle. Number them from 1 to 6 with the silver pen. Cut out a shallow curve between each number, to scallop the edge.

- Talk about how spiders live in webs and look at the pictures. Read the book.

- Go outside and have a web hunt.

- Invite the children to play a game and make a spider's web. Take turns to roll the dice twice and thread a length of ribbon or cord from the first number rolled across the card to the second.

- Repeat until all the holes have been used three or four times and a web made.

- Hang up the webs and add spiders made by the children.

And another idea

Roll a ball or marble covered in white or silver paint across the card circles.

Garden creatures hunt

ELGs: PSED 1; KUW 2, 3, 10; PD 7, 8; CD 1, 2

What you need

- copies of the boards showing six garden creatures, (see page 78) one cut up to make separate cards
- simple information about each one
- paint brushes
- plastic pots
- hand lenses
- large stones around 10cm across
- paper
- paints
- clear, outdoor varnish and laminating materials
- garden canes and string.

What you do

- Pass around the garden creatures cards and find out what the children already know about them. Talk about each one, such as what it is, where it might live, what it eats.

- Explain to the children that they are going on a hunt and that they are looking for the creatures shown on the cards.

- Go into your outdoor area or an outdoor space with a mixture of habitats such as stones, grass area, flowers, plants, logs, leaf litter.

- Show the children how to look carefully in the plants and grass and gently lift up the stones and logs.

- If the children want a closer look, help them use a paintbrush to pick up the creature and place it in a pot. Remind the children to put it back in the same place as they found it.

- Invite the children to make a picture, collage or paint a stone to represent the creatures found. Leave to dry, then laminate or varnish.

- Ask the children to place the pictures and stones where they found the creatures.

And another idea

Plant up tubs or borders with food plants for insects and build an insect hotel to provide winter shelter. The RSPB has instructions for both:

www.rspb.org.uk/advice/gardening/planting/

www.rspb.org.uk/advice/gardening/insects/wildlifestack.aspx

Snails in the lettuce

ELGs: PSED 8; CLL 14, 15; PSRN 1, 2, 3, 9, 11; KUW 1, 2, 3; PD 5, 7, 8

What you need

- recipe and ingredients for cheese scones (see page 79)
- bowl, spoon, scales, baking paper, baking sheet
- oven
- lettuce leaves
- pictures of snails
- snails in a tank with damp soil and lettuce leaves.

What you do

- Look at the snails and the pictures. Watch the snails eating the lettuce and talk about how they like young leaves to eat. Release the snails after watching them.

- Invite the children to make their own snails.

- Following the recipe make the cheese scone dough and share it out.

- Help the children roll it into a long sausage shape. Cut off a piece to make a body and head and help the children wind the remainder into a spiral shape for the shell and place on the body.

- Bake and cool.

- Arrange on a plate with the lettuce leaves, and then eat!

- As the children eat, talk about how savoury foods and salads are a healthy choice.

And another idea

Find out what snails like to eat (for example lettuce, apples, cucumber, cabbages, dandelions, tomatoes) and draw these on to a piece of card. Cut a paper bowl into a spiral and glue along the bowl's rim and secure it to the card, hiding the pictures, making a snail's shell. Draw the body and head on the card. Pull up the snails shell to see what it has eaten!

Clay creature habitats

ELGs: CLL 16, KUW 2, 5, 6, 9, PD 8, CD 2, 3

What you need

- photographs and books of garden creatures in their natural habitats
- air drying clay and modelling tools
- paint

- paper, collage and junk modelling materials
- glue, tape, scissors
- shoe box, or similar, for each child.

What you do

- Talk about where garden creatures live and look at the photos.

- Invite the children to choose a creature and make it out of clay, using the books and photographs as a guide.

- When dry, paint it.

- Remove one long side of the shoe box. Make a habitat landscape in the box from the modelling materials, again helping the children use the books and photographs to find out if the creature lives in grass, amongst flowers or under stones.

- Hide the clay creature in the habitat. Invite the children to see if they can spot where the creatures have been hidden.

And another idea

Hide laminated pictures of garden creatures around the outside area and have a treasure hunt to find them. The prize could be garden stickers or chocolate insects.

The garden shed

ELGs: PSED 2, 12; CLL 14, 7, 8, 11, 16, 17; KUW 8, 9; PD, 8; CD 1, 2, 5

What you need

- story with a garden shed in such as *Mess Monsters in the Garden* by Beth Shoshen (Meadowside Children's Books)
- garden shed role-play items
- sheets or large pieces of card
- wooden shed coloured paint.

What you do

- Talk to the children about who has a shed in their garden and how it is used.

- Read the story to the children. Ask them what they would do to improve the garden after the monsters have been there making a terrible mess.

- Using the children's ideas, make a role-play garden and garden shed using resources such as: children's garden tools, lawnmowers, seed packets, compost, pots, seed trays, wellies, coats, hats, watering cans and a seat. Use decking tiles, stepping stones, green and brown fabric or carpet to represent grass and soil.

- Paint the sheets or card to represent the shed and use as a backdrop.

- Invite the children to act out the story, being the monsters and the people in the story.

- Encourage the children to make up their own garden adventures.

- Provide plenty of writing opportunities such as seed labels, seed packet making, garden notebooks and order forms.

And another idea

Turn the children's ideas into story books, helping them to take photographs, draw pictures and write the story.

Old Macdonald's farm

ELGs: PSED 2, 3, 5; CLL 4, 5; KUW 9; PD 7; CD 4

What you need

- box of farm animals such as a cow, pig, sheep, horse, duck
- pictures of places where the animals live: shed, barn, sty, field, stable, pond
- washing line
- pegs
- Song 'Old MacDonald Animal Homes' (see page 68).

What you do

- Show the children the animals and explain that they need somewhere to live.

- Introduce the pictures showing the animals homes and name them. Discuss which animals could live there.

- Tie the washing line down low, for example, between two chairs. Help the children peg the pictures on to the washing line.

- Sing the 'Old MacDonald' song using the places on the washing line. As the line 'and in that... (barn) he had a...' is reached takes turns to select an animal that could live there, and place it under the picture.

And another idea

Stand in a circle. Take turns to be different farm animals and move around the outside and inside of the circle like that animal as the following song is sung, naming where the animal lives.

(Tune: 'The farmers in the Den')

The pig is in the sty, the pig is in the sty,
E, I, N, D, O the pig is in the sty!

The pig is out the sty, the pig is out the sty,
E, I, N, D, O the pig is out the sty!

Zoo animals postcards

ELGs: CLL 2, 3, 4, 7, 8, 11, 14, 15, 16, 17, 18, 19;
KUW 29; PD 7; CD 2

What you need

- *Dear Zoo* by Rod Campbell (Puffin)
- books and photographs showing where the animals in the story live
- plain card for postcards.

What you do

- Read the story to the children.

- Suggest that instead of going back to the zoo, the animals decide to go on holiday and find out what it's like in the place they originally came from so the zoo can make them somewhere good to live when they come back.

- Discuss how important it is that zoos give animals a natural environment to suit their needs, for example a penguin and a lion could not live in the same type of environment. The penguin likes cold and water and the lion needs somewhere to keep warm inside when the weather is cold.

- Invite the children to choose an animal from the story and find out what sort of environment they like.

- Use the information to pretend to be the animal, designing and making a postcard to send back to the zoo making suggestions for their new home.

- Have the postcards arrive at the zoo and invite the 'zoo keeper' (adult taking on the role), to read them out.

And another idea

Make shopping lists for the zoo keepers so they know what to buy to improve the enclosures.

Pet shop

ELGs: PSED 1, 8, 9, 10, 12; CLL 1, 7;
PSRN 1, 2, 3, 4, 5, 6, 8, 9; KUW 2, 8

What you need
- visit to a pet shop or pictures.
- role-play items.

What you do

- Visit a pet shop or look at the pictures. Point out the features of a pet shop – the pets for sale, items on the shelves, signs, till, baskets and trolleys.

- Talk about how to make a good home for a pet and why it is important they are properly looked after. Ask children to share their experiences of visiting a pet shop and getting a new pet.

- Show the children the pet shop materials, include things such as soft toy pets, carriers, assorted pet food including dried food to weigh out, scales, bags, pet bowls, baskets, collars, leads, toys, blankets, beds, signs, till, price tags, writing materials and money.

- Invite the children to set up a shop in which to take turns to buy and sell the items to make a good home for their pets.

- Talk about what the children bought and how much they cost.

- Make suggestions to extend the play such as special offers, 2p day and comparing the number of items in the baskets.

And another idea
Ask a parents or carers to bring in their pets and talk about the things they do and buy to look after it properly.

Fish in the bowl spinners

ELGs: KUW 2, 4, 6, 7; PD 8

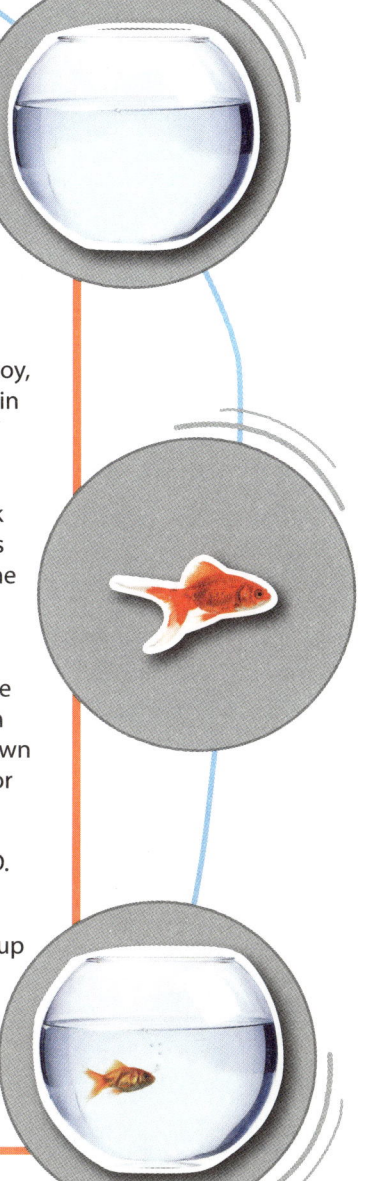

What you need

- pictures of fish in tanks
- old CDs
- computer and printer
- string
- strong tape
- glue
- scissors.

What you do

- Look at the pictures and talk about the different types of fish tanks and bowls.

- Invite the children to make a spinning toy, where the fish magically appears to be in the bowl.

- Help them to cut one metre lengths of string and knot the ends together. Stick on to one side of the CD, so the string is either side of the hole and so there is the same amount of string extending from either side of the CD.

- Use the computer and print off a picture of an empty fish bowl and a smaller fish that will fit on the CD. This could be drawn by the children using a paint program or using clip art or images.

- Glue one picture on each side of the CD. Leave to dry.

- Hold the string in each hand and wind up the CD by turning it over and over.

- Pull both hands apart and watch the fish appear to be in the bowl as the CD spins.

And another idea

Try fish themed online jigsaw puzzles at: www.thekidzpage.com/onlinejigsawpuzzles/ocean_life/index.html

Snake vivariums

ELGs: PSED 1; CLL 3; PSRN 10, 11; KUW 2, 5, 6; PD 7, 8; CD 2

What you need

- pictures of snakes
- card circles around 15cm diameter
- mark making materials
- scissors
- empty, clear plastic washing detergent boxes
- sand
- stones
- Plasticine
- collage and junk modelling materials.

What you do

- Look at the snake pictures. Talk about how their home is often a tank called a vivarium and discuss what they need in there.

- Invite the children to make their own, pretend vivarium.

- Help them to draw a spiral on to the card and cut it out.

- Decorate the card snake with patterns to resemble a real one with pens, paint or collage.

- Place the sand and stones in the plastic box.

- Ask the children what else the snake would need if real and how they could add this to their tank using the materials available.

And another idea

Make snakes from different materials such as Plasticine, salt dough, clay, stuffed tights, bread dough, threaded beads, card tube pieces or paper chains.

Pet kennels

ELGs: PSED 1, 2, 8, 11; CLL 1, 7, 8; PSRN 9;
KUW 2, 8, 9; PD 7; CD 2, 5

What you need

- soft toy pets
- boxes, cages, cat and dog beds, bedding
- food, water and feeding bowls, litter trays
- writing materials, paper, clipboards, registration forms
- uniforms, such as a t-shirt, hat.

What you do

- Invite the children to talk about what happens to their pets when they go on holiday. Where do they live while the family is away?

- Talk about how kennels provide a safe home for pets while their owners are not there to care for them.

- Make up a scenario asking the children to make a kennel for some pets, for example the local one has closed down and the pets booked in have nowhere to go. Ask them what they think they will need.

- Introduce the pet items for them to use and when the kennels are ready start to introduce the soft toy pets.

- Encourage the children to register them, taking down important information and then look after the pet until it is collected.

- Set up a rota of jobs for each day so all the children look after the pets and take turns to feed them, clean them out, play with them or take them for walks.

And another idea

Make a leaflet or poster advertising the new kennels, explaining how the pets will have a 'home from home'.

Little ducklings

ELGs: PSED 3, 5; CLL 3, 4; PSRN 1, 2, 4, 5, 6; PD 2

What you need

- ten plastic ducklings
- blue fabric
- duck mask or headband
- copy of the song 'Ten Little Ducklings' (see page 70).

What you do

- Talk about how ducks live near ponds and rivers, which gives them a good source of food.

- Introduce the song and sing it through.

- Lay out the fabric and ask the children to pick it up holding it along the long edges.

- Invite one child to be mother duck and wear the mask.

- Ask mother duck to place the five ducklings at one of the short ends of the fabric.

- Explain to the children that they have work together as the song is sung to move the ducklings along the fabric river without any falling off, and then get them back to Mother duck when she quacks to show how many need to come back, so three quacks equals three ducklings.

- Change the number of ducklings starting each time.

And another idea

Use paper plates to make duck headbands. Fold one in half and paint for the beak. Glue this to half a plate close to the cut edge. Add eyes peeping out from above the beak and add tufts of wool or feathers at the top. Fasten to a card band. Wear them to act out the duck counting rhymes on pages 70-71.

A river of fish

ELGs: CLL 10, 19; KUW 9; PD 8; CD 2, 3

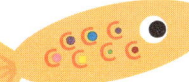

What you need

- clay tiles (for 'And another idea')
- finger paints in blues and greens
- paper
- fine black marker pens
- sequins
- PVA glue
- cotton buds
- pictures and books of fish that live in local rivers.

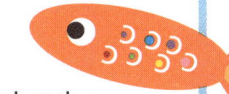

What you do

- Talk about how fish live in rivers and streams. Look at the pictures.

- Spread the paint on a plastic table, wipe-clean cloth or tray.

- Invite the child to draw lines through the paint with their fingers to represent the movement of the water.

- Place the paper on top to make a print. Leave to dry.

- Using the pen, draw fish in the river, decorating the fish with repeated letters to make patterns to represent the scales for example c c c c, or d d d d.

- Using the cotton bud, place a dab of glue inside each scale and add a sequin.

And another idea

Make a frieze of clay tiles depicting the river, with each child using modelling tools to draw on the patterns found in moving water. Glaze or paint and cover in PVA glue or varnish.

Pond life counting

ELGs: PSED 5, 13, 14; CLL 11, 17, 18, 19;
PSRN 1, 2, 3; KUW 2, 6, 9; CD 3

What you need

- blue or white paper
- blue paint mixed with water and washing up liquid
- blue and green tissue-paper
- glue
- drinking straws
- collage materials
- pictures and books showing pond life.

What you do

- Look at the pictures of the pond life and talk about the wide variety of creatures that live in or near the pond.

- Ask the children to think of their favourite creatures and write (or draw) these as a 'top ten'.

- Invite the children to put these into a counting book or a frieze from 0 showing an empty pond, then each page depicting their 'top ten', for example: 1 with one frog, 2 with two newts and so on.

- Make a page for each number by blowing in the blue paint with a straw and making a bubble print for the pond. Add torn blue tissue strips for the rippling water and green for the weeds.

- Using the pictures and books as guides, make the creatures from collage for example, bubble wrap newts, drinking straw pond skaters and foil fish.

- Help the children arrange them on the pages and add the numeral to show how many there are, together with the name of the creature.

- Put them in number order and make into a book or frieze.

And another idea

Make a simple column graph to show the children's favourite pond creatures, asking them to stick on a picture in the corresponding column. Count how many in each column and find the favourite.

Dancing jellyfish

ELGs: PD 1, 2; KUW 1, 2, 7; PD 1, 2, 4, 8; CD 1, 2, 4, 5

What you need

- video clip of jellyfishes moving or photographs
- sea music to dance to such as 'Fingal's Cave' by Mendelssohn or sea sounds
- a plastic bowl or the bottom part of a 2l drinks bottle
- ribbon
- bubble wrap and crêpe paper in 2 cm wide strips
- double sided tape.

What you do

- Watch the video together or look at the photos and talk about how jellyfish live in the sea. Look at how they move through the sea, their colour and transparency and how many tentacles they have.

- Play the sea music and watch them move again.

- Invite the children to make their own jellyfish by placing the tape on the inside of the bottle bottom or bowl and attaching different materials for tentacles.

- Make a hole in the centre of each bowl. Thread a length of ribbon through the hole and tie a large knot on the inside.

- Play the music and encourage the children to move the jellyfish as if they are moving through the sea.

And another idea

Hang the jellyfish up alongside strips of green and blue cellophane as part of an under the sea mobile or hanging display.

Undersea worlds

ELGs: PSED 1, KUW 2, 5, 6, 9; PD 8; CD 2, 3, 5

What you need

- books and pictures of life in the sea
- small boxes or shoe boxes with one long side removed
- sandpaper, sand, shells, stones
- blue and clear cellophane
- Plasticine
- pictures of creatures found in the sea
- collage materials
- thread, sticky tape.

What you do

- Ask the children to name all the creatures they can think of that live in the sea. Add to the list using the books. Talk about some being easier to see like crabs and shellfish and some that live so deep they are rarely seen.

- Invite the children to make an undersea world in a box.

- Use the sandpaper, sand, shells and stones to make the sea bed and cover the sides in blue cellophane.

- Make weed from the Plasticine.

- Arrange the pictures of the creatures or ask the children to draw their own or make them from collage materials. Suspend those that swim from the roof of the box with thread.

- Cover the front of the box with clear cellophane.

And another idea

Cover the top of the box to look like the sea and waves. Make boats, people and birds to go in the waves and perhaps a mermaid or two!

An island home

ELGs: PSED 3, 12; CLL 1, 2, 4, 7, 5, 6, 9;
PD 1, 2, 3, 8; CD 2, 3, 5

What you need

- island stories such as the Katie Morag series by Mairi Hedderwick (Red Fox)
- large area of blue plastic, fabric or carpet
- plain rugs and cushions
- tent covered in fabric
- large appliance box to turn into a boat and 'boat building' materials
- writing materials
- treasure such as shells, pebbles with letters on, gemstones.

What you do

- Read one of the stories and talk about what life would be like on an island.

- Make the rugs and cushions into an island by placing them on the large area of blue plastic, fabric or carpet. Introduce it to the children and explain that they need to find a way to get to the island, as in the story.

- Help them make a boat using the large appliance box and 'boat building' materials such as a long tube for a mast, card to make oars , fabric for a sail.

- When they have a boat to reach the island set a daily challenge in addition to playing there. This could be shells to find and sort, making words from the letter pebbles or finding treasure using a map.

- Ask them for ideas of things to add to the island and games to play there.

And another idea

Use the island as a relaxation area and provide soothing sea sounds for the children to listen to.

Woodland world

ELGs: PSED 2, 8, 11; CLL 1, 7; PSRN 12;
KUW 2, 3, 5, 8, 9, 10; CD 2, 5

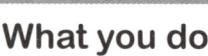

What you need

- video clips, poster and books about woodlands (try the Woodland Trust)
- builders tray or sandpit
- compost, chipped bark
- pots of tiny trees, ferns, grasses and plants (check they are not poisonous)
- shallow container and water
- moss, dead leaves, twigs, small branches, stones, acorns, conkers
- small world wildlife animals.

What you do

- Talk about what a woodland is and share experiences of visiting one. Explain how a wide variety of animals live there, in the ground, under stones, under fallen leaves and in trees.

- Look at the information resources.

- Encourage the children to work together to make a miniature woodland. Remind them to wash their hands after playing with the woodland and not to put anything in their mouth.

- Cover the tray in a thick layer of compost and bark. Plant the trees and small plants and make a pool with the shallow container. Arrange the stones, twigs and other resources.

- Introduce the small world animals such as birds, rabbits, deer, badgers, butterflies, owls, hedgehogs and invite the children to make up stories about living in the woodland.

And another idea

Make a woodland senses area with natural resources such as twigs, pine cones, chestnuts and bark for the children to smell and touch.

Burrows and holes sound game

ELGs: CLL 2, 3, 4, 9, 10; KUW 2; PD 2

What you need

- finger rhyme 'Rabbit Holes' (see page 72)
- pictures of animals that live in holes, burrows or dens
- items beginning with the same initial sound as the animals for example 'r' - radish, rat, ribbon, rope plus some that don't
- extra large boxes or children's tents
- earth coloured fabric or paper.

What you do

- Share the rabbit rhyme with the children and do the actions.

- Talk about animals that live in holes such as a rabbits, mice, badgers and foxes. Discuss how some have special names such as a burrow, warren or den. Explain that these are safe, dry and warm places to live.

- Cover extra large boxes or children's tents in earth coloured fabric or paper to be animal homes. Spread the items around the homes. Show the children the box or tent homes and the items.

- Explain to the children that the animals that live in these homes can only take things inside that start with the same initial sound.

- Place an animal picture next to each tent and invite the children to match the items to the correct home and place them inside.

And another idea

Draw the same letters in large upper and lower case script on the ground. Invite the children to hop along the R and r like a rabbit or scurry like a mouse along the M and m.

Polar bear cave game

ELGs: PSED 3, 7, 8; PSED 1, 2, 3, 4, 7; KUW 2, 9; PD 9

What you need

- photographs or video clips of mother polar bear and cubs on the ice and in their hole
- photograph of adult polar bear in an ice cave
- large piece of pale blue card
- white stickers
- polar bear pictures
- counters or blocks
- a dice.

What you do

- Look at the photographs or video of the mother polar bear and cubs on the ice and in their hole. Talk about how the mother bear makes this home ready for her new cubs, staying there until winter ends.

- Make up a game board by placing the photograph in the centre of the board. Make four paths from the corners, leading to the photograph, using the stickers to represent pieces of ice. Ensure each path has the same number of stickers.

- Make polar bear cub counters by sticking a picture to a counter or block.

- Invite the children to roll the dice and move that number of ice pieces along the board to help their cub get back to mum in the snow hole. Play until all the cubs are safe.

And another idea

Make cards linked to polar bear facts, such as 'see a seal and chase it, go back 3' or 'ice block moves in the water, move on 1'. Mark some of the stickers with a polar bear footprint. If a cub meets one of these they take a card and follow what it says.

Hibernation holes

ELGs: PSED 3; CLL 3, 5, 16

What you need

- dried leaves, grass, straw
- plastic creatures which hibernate such as bats, snakes, frogs, hedgehogs, tortoises
- rhyme 'Winter Sleep' (see page 68)
- books about hibernation
- salt dough
- paints
- small pots and boxes.

What you do

- Place a mound of leaves and dry grass on the floor. Hide the plastic animals in the leaves.

- Sit with the children around the mound and talk about how we stay warm for winter in our homes.

- Explain that animals get ready for winter by finding a place to live that is warm and dry and going into a very deep sleep until Spring called hibernation.

- Share the rhyme with the children.

- Tell the children that under the leaves are creatures that hibernate for them to find.

- After the hunt, look in the books to find out where these animals hibernate.

- Make models of these animals from the salt dough. Paint when dry.

- Encourage the children to make a hibernation place, the right size for their creature, using the pots and boxes and add bedding to make it warm.

And another idea

Use the 'Winter Sleep' rhyme (see page 68) to pretend to be the animals getting ready to hibernate. Provide animal masks, a large area and materials with which to build winter homes.

Little Lion's first walk

ELGs: PSED 2; PD 1, 2, 3, 4

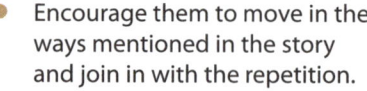

What you need

- materials for an obstacle course
- Copy of Little Lion's first walk on page 66.

What you do

- Talk to the children about how animals living in the wild face challenges in their everyday life. The place where they live is full of hazards, for example other animals, things to climb over or run around.

- Set up an obstacle course, linked to the story with the challenges Little Lion meets. For example: space to move as the lion cub; logs to run through; piles of sticks or branches to jump over; a blue fabric river with carpet tile rocks to hop on; a plank to slither over and a tunnel to go through into the den.

- Invite the children to pretend to be Little Lion by tackling the challenges and reaching the safety of the den.

- Encourage them to move in the ways mentioned in the story and join in with the repetition.

And another idea

Act out a story based on how animals move such as *Walking Through the Jungle* by Julie Lacome (Walker) or *The Animal Boogie* by Debbie Harter (Barefoot Books Ltd).

Henri Rousseau's jungle

ELGs: CLL 8; KUW 9; CD 1, 2, 3, 5

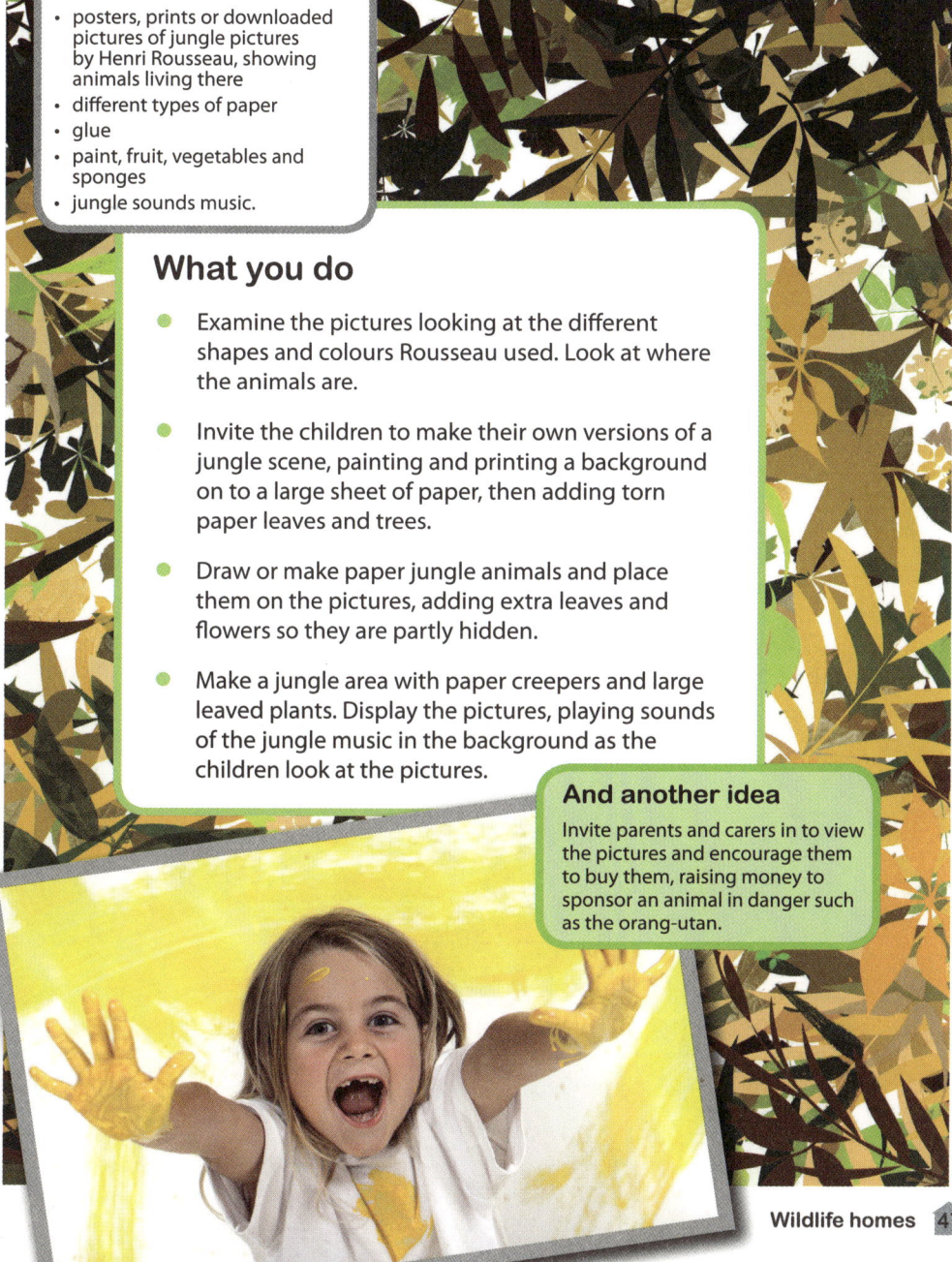

What you need

- posters, prints or downloaded pictures of jungle pictures by Henri Rousseau, showing animals living there
- different types of paper
- glue
- paint, fruit, vegetables and sponges
- jungle sounds music.

What you do

- Examine the pictures looking at the different shapes and colours Rousseau used. Look at where the animals are.

- Invite the children to make their own versions of a jungle scene, painting and printing a background on to a large sheet of paper, then adding torn paper leaves and trees.

- Draw or make paper jungle animals and place them on the pictures, adding extra leaves and flowers so they are partly hidden.

- Make a jungle area with paper creepers and large leaved plants. Display the pictures, playing sounds of the jungle music in the background as the children look at the pictures.

And another idea

Invite parents and carers in to view the pictures and encourage them to buy them, raising money to sponsor an animal in danger such as the orang-utan.

Owl babies

ELGs: PSED 4, 5, 13, 14; CLL 2, 4, 6, 7, 8; CD 2

What you need

- *Owl Babies* by Martin Waddell (Walker)
- cotton wool balls
- glue
- stickers
- long piece of bark or a branch.

What you do

- Read the story about the baby owls in the nest, worried that their mummy will not come back.

- Talk about how the mummy bird has to leave them to go and find food.

- Think about how the baby birds might have felt.

- Using the cotton wool balls make baby owls by gluing then together. Tease out the edges of the balls to give a feathery look. Add eyes and beaks made from the stickers.

- Place them on the branch.

- Invite the children to tell the birds about times they have been afraid or scared or felt alone, but it was alright in the end.

And another idea

Make finger puppet birds and sing the rhyme 'Two Little Dicky Birds', making the birds fly away, but then come back again.

Pop-up chicks

ELGs: PSED 3; CLL 9, 10, 12, 14

What you need

- card chick shapes
- glue
- feathers
- googly eyes
- mini clothes pegs
- plant canes
- clean yoghurt pots
- paints
- letters of the alphabet (initial sounds) written on oval pieces of card.

What you do

- With the children, make some pop-up chicks by covering the chick shapes with feathers and adding googly eyes. Use a mini clothes peg for the beak. Fasten a cane to each one.

- Paint the yoghurt pots to represent eggs and make a slit in the base of each one. Pop the chicks in to the yoghurt pots so the canes go through the hole.

- Fasten a letter into each beak, so a word can be made. Lower the chicks into the eggs.

- Invite three or four children to hold a chick and slowly pop up the letters one at a time.

- Name the letters.

- Challenge the children to rearrange the chicks so the letters make a word.

And another idea

Write simple words on to cards to put in the beaks. Using a bird puppet, say a sentence, for example 'I am a cat', and challenge the children to find the words and put them in order in the chick's beaks.

Egg tangrams

ELGs: PSRN 11, 12; PD 8; CD 3, 5

What you need

- copies of the egg tangram (see page 80)
- scissors
- digital camera and printer.

What you do

- Talk about how all birds hatch out of eggs, but each breed of bird is different, with different coloured feathers, size and shape.

- Show the children the egg-shaped tangram and invite them to cut it up into the different shapes, naming them.

- Show the children how to rearrange the shapes to make different birds and invite them to try.

- Take photographs and print off copies.

- Challenge the children to try to make the birds in the photographs.

And another idea

Make printed bird pictures with shape sponges and paint.

Feeding the garden birds

ELGs: PSED 1; KUW 2; PD 8

What you need

- copy of the song on page 69
- pine cone
- string
- peanut butter
- teaspoon
- bird seed in a bowl.

What you do

- Talk about how birds live in gardens. Explain to the children that we can encourage them to make their home there by feeding them.

- Sing the action song about feeding the birds, making the actions.

- Invite the children to make pine cone treats for the birds.

- Tie a length of string to the top of the pine cone.

- Spread the peanut butter (check for nut allergies first) all over the cone, pushing it down into the gaps with the teaspoon handle.

- Roll the cone in the bird seed.

- Hang up and watch the birds come to feed off the cone.

And another idea

Identify the birds that come and find out what they like to eat, then make treats or put out food for them.

Make a nest

ELGs: PSED 2; KUW 1, 2, 3, 4, 5, 9; PD 8

What you need
- books and photographs of nests
- nest-building materials
- tweezers
- spoons
- small jugs and pots
- water.

What you do

- Explain that a nest is a bird's home, a place to lay eggs and care for the chicks. Talk to the children about where birds build their nests and how they choose places that are safe from the weather and predators such as other birds, cats and people.

- Have a close look at the nest pictures. How have they been made and what is used in the centre of the nest?

- Invite the children to make a nest, reminding them that a bird only carries one thing at a time and can only use their beak! Provide materials such as feathers, thin twigs, leaves, straw, grass, sheep's wool, soil, mud and compost.

- Suggest that they might like to try with tweezers first then use spoons.

- Allow the children ample time to work on their nests so they can change or add to the design and experiment with mud-making.

- When finished compare their nests with the pictures and talk about the building experience.

- Suggest the children put their nests in safe places outside.

And another idea
Weave materials suitable for nesting through mesh and hang outside. Watch what the birds take.

Home for a lost bird!

ELGs: PSED 1, 2, 4, 8, 12, 13, 14; CLL 1, 2, 3, 7, 8, 17; KUW 5, 6

What you need

- very large toy bird or puppet
- letter
- materials to make a bird home
- writing materials.

Hello

I am lost and need a new home. Can you help me please?

Tweety xx

What you do

- Place the bird with a letter from it (explaining that it has got lost and needs help making a home) where the children will find it.

- Read the letter and ask the children for suggestions of what to do.

- Go with the suggestions, but use more letters from the bird to guide how they look after it, perhaps by saying the nest was nice but I got wet when it rained, or I get very hungry at night when no one is here.

- Use the letters to guide the children's thinking and research skills as well as introducing new play and learning experiences.

- Suggest that the children write notes back to the bird.

- When the children are ready, send the bird a plane ticket for its journey home and a letter asking them to make a safe travelling crate.

- Make a book of the children's experiences as the activity progresses.

And another idea

Introduce short-term bird visitors of different sizes and from different places such as water, sandy desert or rainforests and ask the children to make a suitable place for them to live in while visiting.

Tents

ELGs: PSED 2, 5, 6, 13; CLL 1, 7, 8;
KUW 5, 6, 8, 11; PD 7, 8

What you need

- photos of tent-based homes (such as yurts, teepees, lavuu-Sami tent from Lapland)
- pictures of camping tents
- plain sheets or large pieces of fabric
- paints
- string
- chairs
- broom handles
- food.

What you do

- Show the children the photographs of the tent-based homes from around the world. Ask if they know what they are called.

- Explain to the children that traditionally tent-like homes were used to provide shelter for people who moved around frequently, such as nomads and animal herders, as they were quick to put up and could be carried around from place to place.

- Look at the modern tents and ask for the children's experiences of using one.

- Invite the children to work in small groups to design and make a tent that they and a friend can fit inside, using the fabric for the cover and then deciding how they can get it to stay up.

- Decorate the fabric with paint.

- When dry put up the tents, using the pictures to gain information about the different ways the structure of the tent is made.

- Set up camp for the day and eat camp food, play outdoor games and sing songs.

And another idea

Read stories about camping for the children to re-tell in their tent, act out or to inspire role-play, such as *Maisie Goes Camping* by Lucy Cousins. (Walker).

Space station

ELGs: PSED 1, 11, 12; CLL 4, 5, 7, 16;
KUW 4, 5, 6, 7; CD 2, 3, 5

What you need

- space story such as *The Man on the Moon* by Simon Bartram (Templar Publishing)
- pictures of space travel
- cardboard boxes, packaging and craft materials
- two-litre drinks bottles
- duck tape
- wide elastic
- wellies
- t-shirts with a space logo sprayed or painted on.

What you do

- Read the story with the children and talk about what is in space and on the moon. *The Man on the Moon* is a story about Bob, who works on the moon as his day job and thinks that there is no such thing as aliens.

- Look at the pictures and space resources.

- Invite the children to build their own space station or rocket using the materials available, such as boxes and packaging, silver foil, fabric, paint and grey pipe insulation.

- Make air tanks by fastening two plastic two-litre bottles together with duck tape and make shoulder straps from elastic. Spray them with silver paint and wear with wellies!

- Make alien head bands with materials such as card, straws, pom-poms, paper balls and googly eyes.

- Encourage the children to put on the clothes and make up stories about travelling in space and being on the moon. Some might like to act out being Bob in the story, with others being aliens.

And another idea

Make models of aliens using recyclable materials to hide around the space role-play area.

Make a lighthouse game

ELGs: PSED 6, 8, PSRN 1, 2, 3, 4, 5; KUW 9

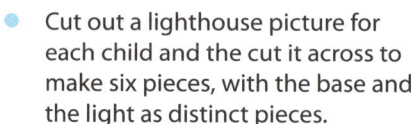
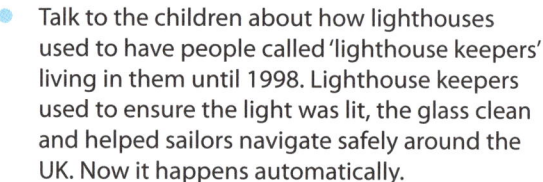

What you need

- simple lighthouse pictures
- dice
- plain paper
- paint
- collage materials
- glue.

What you do

- Cut out a lighthouse picture for each child and the cut it across to make six pieces, with the base and the light as distinct pieces.

- Number the pieces from 1 to 6, with the base being 1 and the light 6.

- Talk to the children about how lighthouses used to have people called 'lighthouse keepers' living in them until 1998. Lighthouse keepers used to ensure the light was lit, the glass clean and helped sailors navigate safely around the UK. Now it happens automatically.

- Introduce the 'Build a lighthouse' game. Give each child a set of pieces and invite them to take turns to roll the dice and build their lighthouse. This could be played in a variety of ways, for example rolling a 1 to start and a 6 to end or rolling and collecting the pieces in any order.

- Glue the completed lighthouse on to paper and add the sea and rocks around it, using paint, paper or collage.

And another idea

Make a lighthouse with twelve pieces. Roll two dice, with the children choosing to use one of the numbers rolled or adding them together to get the pieces.

Troglodyte houses

ELGs: PSED 13, 3; CLL 5; KUW 1, 6, 9, 11; PD 8; CD 2, 3

What you need

- photographs of troglodyte houses
- clay
- modelling tools.

What you do

- Look at the pictures of the houses and explain to the children how long ago people all over the world carved these homes, which went deep into soft rocks, such as chalk or sandstone. They were a safe place to live, hidden from enemies and well insulated so they stayed the same temperature all the year round. Talk about how now people still live in them and stay in them for a holiday.

- Introduce the clay and let the children explore what they can do with it.

- Invite the children to make a troglodyte house from the clay, using the photos as guidance. This could be a model showing the layout or what it looks like from the outside.

And another idea

Mix cornflour into dry sand to improve the building qualities of the sand. Add water until damp. Invite the children to make tunnels and underground rooms, seeing how deep or large they can make them before they collapse.

Dinosaur swamp

ELGs: PSED 1, 5, 8, 12; CLL 7; KUW 1, 9; PD 8; CD 1, 2, 3, 5

What you need

- pictures of dinosaur swamps
- swamp water: warm water, washing-up liquid, pure soap flakes, green paint
- bucket or large mixing bowl
- hand rotary whisk
- shallow water tray
- stones, twigs, sand, compost, logs, leaves, small plants
- plastic dinosaurs.

What you do

- Explain to the children that a very long time ago there were dinosaurs and that some lived in swamps.

- Look at the pictures to see how a swamp is different from other environments.

- Invite the children to make their own dinosaur swamp.

- Help them to make swamp water by whisking all the ingredients together in the bucket until thick. Pour into the tray outside.

- Encourage the children to make a place for the dinosaurs to live by adding in the other materials.

- Add the dinosaurs and make up stories.

And another idea

Find out about animals currently living in swamps such as alligators, fish, frogs, birds and introduce plastic models of these for when the dinosaurs die out and become extinct.

Castle skittles

ELGs: PSED 2; CLL 5; PSRN 11, 12; KUW 3, 9; PD 2, 7, 8; CD 2, 3

What you need

- pictures of castles
- paint
- paper
- items that will print different shapes –sponges, boxes, bricks, lids
- large cereal boxes
- soft balls.

What you do

- Look at the pictures of castles, identifying the different shapes found in the castles and the way the height of the towers, turrets and walls vary.

- Talk about who used to live in a castle and how they were strong safe places against attack from enemies, and who lives in them now.

- Invite the children to use the items to print their own castle designs, applying paint carefully to the item and placing it on the paper so it makes a clean print.

- When dry cut out and glue to the cereal boxes.

- Line the castles up and invite the children to try and knock down the 'enemy' castles by throwing the balls at them.

And another idea

Make bricks to build castles with by filling small food pots, tins and individual cereal boxes (lined with cling film), with concrete, made up from a bag of pre-mixed dry powder. When set make towers and buildings.

Noah's ark

ELGs: PSED 3, 8; CLL 4, 13; PSRN 1, 2

What you do

- Read the story of Noah's ark and talk about how Noah built the animals a new place to live so they were safe from the flood.

- Make an ark from a long painted box such as a shoe box, and with one short end cut to make a drop down ramp. Place some hay in the ark.

- Put the animals in the bag. Invite the children to take an animal from the bag and name it.

- Explain that the animals need to get in the ark, but they can't all go at once they need to take turns.

- Introduce the rhyme 'The animals went in two by two. Who has got the... (tigers)... one and two!'

- Ask each pair of children to carefully put their animals in the ark, as the animals are mentioned, until the ark is full.

- Re-tell the rest of the story together and take the animals out of the ark in pairs at the end.

What you need

- Noah's ark story, such as *Noah's Ark* by Lucy Cousins (Walker Books)
- plastic zoo and farm animals (two of each)
- bag
- shoe box
- paints
- scissors
- hay

And another idea

Make a rainbow by printing pairs of hands on to a long piece of plain wallpaper.

Fairy tale castle

ELGs: PSED 2, 5; CLL 1, 4; PSRN 1, 2, 3, 5, 7, 9, 10, 11;
PD 2, 4, 8; CD 2, 3, 4

What you need

- pictures of fairy tale castles
- rhyme 'There Was a Princess Long-a-go'
- assorted cardboard boxes
- paint
- glittery and sparkly craft materials cut into shapes
- 1-6 dice
- + and – dice
- small world figures.

What you do

- Sing and act out the rhyme together.

- Ask the children to imagine that the prince and princess go to live in a fairytale castle. What would it look like? Share their ideas with each other and then look at the pictures.

- Invite the children to paint and decorate the boxes with the shapes, naming them and encouraging them to make patterns. Explain that the boxes will be used to build a castle. Leave to dry.

- Take turns to roll the dice and add or take off the corresponding number of boxes to build a fairytale castle. Compare the size and height of the towers being built.

- Make up stories about who might live in the castle and re-tell them using small world figures.

And another idea

Provide large appliance boxes and smaller cartons to make a castle the children can build and sit in.

A home in a tree

ELGs: PSED 4, 5; CLL 4; KUW 2, 6, 9, 10; CD 2, 4

What you need

- *After the Storm* by Nick Butterworth (HarperCollins Children's Books)
- large sheets of brown paper
- green paper
- dark wax crayons
- leaves and paint
- pictures of the animals in the story and others that live in, on or under trees

What you do

- Share the story with the children – the animals lose their homes because the tree they live in and under blows down in a storm. Look at how Percy helps the animals find somewhere new to live.

- Talk about fallen trees the children have seen and how they felt about these.

- Invite the children to make a giant tree like the one in the story to show where the animals used to live before the storm.

- To make the trunk and branches of the tree, make bark rubbings on the brown paper with the wax crayons.

- Make leaf prints with the paint and make leaf rubbings with wax crayons, then cut out the leaves.

- Assemble the tree on a wall adding twisted brown paper to represent the roots.

- Use spare bark rubbings and leaves to make doors to open and flaps to lift.

- Behind the doors, hide the creatures that live in the tree.

- Cut strips of green paper to resemble grass and place at the base of the tree. Hide pictures of creatures that live at the base amongst the blades of grass.

And another idea

Use musical and home-made instruments to add a sound track to the story for the rain, wind, thunder, paddling across the water in the wheel barrow and Percy making new homes.

Inside the eggs!

ELGs: PSED 1; CLL 4; PSRN 1, 2, 9, 11; PD 8

What you need
- *Meg's Eggs* by Jan Pienkowski (Puffin)
- dough ingredients
- small toy dinosaurs
- small hammer, metal spoon, blunt knife, paint brush
- safety goggles.

What you do

- Make dinosaur eggs in a variety of different sizes. Mix together the ingredients and make a dough. Give a piece of dough to each child and show them how to make an egg shape with a toy dinosaur hidden inside. Ensure the dinosaurs are well covered in dough. Bake the 'eggs' for 30-40 minutes at 170°C until the outside is hard and dry. Leave to cool.

- Hide the eggs.

- Read the story of Meg's Eggs. In the story Meg tries to conjure up eggs for tea but they hatch out in the night to reveal dinosaurs.

- Invite the children to go on their own egg hunt, counting how many they find.

- Sort the eggs into size order.

- Show the children the equipment for opening the eggs and invite them to see what is hidden inside. This can be messy so cracking open the eggs in a tray will help contain the mess!

- When all the dinosaurs are found encourage the children to find different ways of sorting them such as by size or colour.

Dough recipe

What you need:
- 1 cup plain flour
- 1 cup used dried out coffee grounds
- ½ cup salt
- ¼ cup sand
- ¾ cup water.

What to do:
Mix together all the ingredients until they form a soft dough.

And another idea
Use the same mixture to make sets of model dinosaurs each a different size.

Home pop-ups

ELGs: CLL 4; KUW 2, 6; PD 1, 2, 4, 8; CD 2, 3

What you need

- pictures of a nest, hive and rabbit hole
- rhyme 'Animal Homes' (see page 71)
- yoghurt pot and individual sized cereal boxes
- 30cm dowel
- card
- straw
- paint
- fabric
- glue or tape
- scissors

What you do

● Show the children the pictures of a nest, hive and rabbit hole and ensure they know what they are.

● Share the rhyme with the children, encouraging them to join in with the actions.

● Ask them to choose their favourite line in the action rhyme.

● Invite them to make a pop-up toy for that line.

● For the nest and hole use a yoghurt pot for the base and for the house use a cereal box. Make a hole in the base of each, through which to put the dowel. For the hive use the yoghurt pot upside down, so the bee pops out of the bottom. Decorate these to look like the home adding paint, fabric or a drawn picture.

● Make the creature or person from card and decorate with the paint and fabric. Secure to the dowel with glue or tape.

● Push the end of the dowel through the hole in the pot or box, from the inside so the creature or person is hidden. Push the dowel up to reveal the hidden bird, rabbit and person and down to reveal the bee.

● Repeat the rhyme and use the pop-up toys on the appropriate lines.

And another idea

Share some of the finger rhymes based on animal homes in the rhymes section on pages 69-73

Going to build a house

ELGs: PSED 2; CLL 2, 4; PSRN 11; KUW 6; PD 8; CD 3, 4

What you need

- song 'Going to Build a House' (see page 69)
- large cardboard appliance boxes
- cardboard cut from spare boxes
- paint, foil, clear plastic, wallpaper
- pieces of carpet
- scissors
- glue, tape.

What you do

- Sing the song to the children, then help them to sing it with you so they become familiar with the words.

- Suggest they follow the lines of the song and make their own houses from the boxes, painting them and adding materials to make their dream house.

- Remind the children of the lines in the song as they work and help with cutting and attaching materials as necessary.

- When the houses are complete arrange them as a village, for the children to play in.

And another idea

Design and colour in a house on line at: www.bobthebuilder.com/uk/games_design_a_house.asp

Little Lion's First Walk

Little Lion woke up and scampered out of the den. He looked around, but no one was there. That's odd he thought I wonder where they are, I think I will go and find them.

He set off slowly at first but then quicker and quicker until he was nearly running. But then he stopped, suddenly. He remembered he had never been out on his own before. He thought for a moment, 'They can't be far away' he said to himself and carried on.

Soon he came to some logs lying across the track. 'Oh no!' he said 'What long heavy logs. I can't go under them and I can't go around them, I know I'll step over them! Step, step, step, step.'

And he carried on along the track.

Soon he came to some branches lying across the track. 'Oh no!' he said 'What a jumble of branches. I can't go under them and I can't go around them, I know I'll jump over them! Jump, jump, jump, jump.'

And he carried on along the track.

Soon he came to a river running across the track. 'Oh no!' he said 'What a deep cold river. I can't go under it and I can't go around it, I know I'll use the rocks! Hop, hop, hop, hop.'

And he carried on along the track.

Soon he came to a hole across the track. 'Oh no!' he said 'What a deep hole. I can't go under it and I can't go around it, I know I'll use the log and slither across it! Slither, slither, slither, slither.'

And he carried on along the track.

In front of him was a tunnel. Little Lion went to investigate. He crawled along the tunnel, slowly and carefully and found himself inside a dark hole. He heard a growl and felt a paw on his tail.

A voice came out of the dark. 'Little Lion come here. You are too little to go out alone!'

The paw scooped up Little Lion and tucked him back in bed.

Little Lion kept quiet about going out alone!

Old MacDonald Animal Homes

Old MacDonald had a barn E I E I O
And in that barn he had a pig E I E I O.
With an 'oink oink' here and an 'oink oink' there,
Here an 'oink', there an 'oink', everywhere an
'oink oink'.
Old Macdonald had a barn E I E I O.

*Change the animal home for each new verse to
include shed, barn, sty, field, stable or pond.*

Winter Sleep

(Tune: Twinkle, Twinkle Little Star)

Hurry animals, don't be slow
Winter's coming, close to you.
Run and scamper all around
Collecting bedding from the ground.
Hurry animals, snuggle in deep
Winter's coming, time to sleep.

Going to Build a House

Going to build a house,
Going to build a house,
With a chimney tall.
With a chimney tall.
Going to build a roof,
Going to build a roof,
And a garden wall.
And a garden wall.
And a big front door you can open wide.
Two small windows you can peep inside.
Going to build a house,
Going to build a house.
We're going to build a house.

Feed the Birds
(Tune: Row, Row, Row Your Boat)

Feed, feed, feed the birds
(use thumb and two fingers to peck at food)
Feed them all year round.
(draw a circle shape in the air with finger)
Put out water, sprinkle seed
(cup one hand, with other pretend to pick up the seed and sprinkle it)
And watch them fly around.
(link hands at thumbs, move hands up and down, as if birds flying)

My Little House

My little house won't stand up straight.
My little house has lost its gate.
My little house bends up and down.
My little house is the oldest in the town.
Here comes the wind to blow and blow again.
Down falls my little house. Oh what a shame!

Ten Little Ducklings

Ten little ducklings,
Off in a flash!
Jump in the river,
Splash, splash, splash!

Along comes mother duck,
'Quack, quack, quack!'
How many ducklings
come swimming back?

Mother duck quacks how many. Change the starting number each time

Five Yellow Ducks

Five yellow ducks went out to play

(wiggle five fingers on one hand)

And met a white duck on the way.

(wiggle one finger on other hand)

The five yellow ducks went to get a snack

(put hand behind back)

And the one white duck went quack, quack, quack.

(use hand to form duck beak and quack)

Change the number of yellow and white ducks each time.

Five Little Ducks

Five little ducks, went out one day

(hold up five fingers)

over the hills, and far away,

(hold hand to eyebrows)

Mother duck said 'Quack Quack Quack'

(motion 'quack' with your hand)

And four little ducks came waddling back.

(make wings with arms and move elbows up and down)

Continue to count down until there are no little ducks then sing:

No little ducks went out to play,

Over the hills and far away,

Then father duck said 'QUACK, QUACK, QUACK',

And five little ducks came waddling back.

Animal Homes

Here is a nest for a robin,

(cup hands)

Here is a hive for a bee.

(make a fist and wrap other hand around it)

Here is a hole for a bunny,

(make circle with hands)

And here is a house for me!

(put arms above head with fingers touching like a roof)

Rabbit Holes

Here is a rabbit, with soft brown ears,

(raise two fingers)

And here is a hole in the ground.

(make hole with fingers of other hand)

She hears a sound, and pricks up her ears,

(straighten fingers)

And pops right into the ground.

(put fingers in hole)

Five Little Birds

Five little birds without a home,

(raise five fingers of left hand)

Five little trees in a row.

(raise right hand high over head)

Here come the birds to build their nests

(cup right hand and fly left hand fingers into it)

Up in the branches tall.

(hold both hands above head and wiggle fingers)

Here is a Bee Hive

Here is the beehive. Where are the bees?

(hold up fist and shake)

Hidden away where nobody sees.

(move other hand around fist)

Watch and you'll see them come out of the hive

(bend head close to fist)

One, two, three, four, five.

(hold fingers up one at a time)

Buzz, buzz, buzz, buzz, buzz….all fly away!

(wiggle fingers)

ICT resources and ideas

General

ELGs: PSED 6; KUW 2, 7, 9, 10, 11

Website: www.kids.nationalgeographic.com/kids/

- Fantastic site for children with lots of games, activities, facts and video footage about all sorts of creatures, people and places, science, space, history and more.

Website: www.visitbritain.com/en/GB/

- Excellent photographs of places around Britain.

Homes around the world

ELGs: PSED 6; KUW 3, 7, 9, 10, 11

Website: www.warrinerprimaries.com/Topic/homesworld.htm

- Homes around the world game. Match the homes to reveal the treasure.

Website: www.hgpho.to/wfest/house/house-e.html

- Photographs of homes around the world with simple information about where they are found and how they are made.

Website: www.designboom.com/contemporary/tiny_houses.html

- Ideas for complete houses on a tiny scale.

Animals and birds

ELGs: KUW 2, 3, 4, 7, 9, 10

Website:www.animal.discovery.com/animals/

- Information on all sorts of animals: pets, zoo and wild animals, insects, fish and birds plus a section on imaginary and prehistoric life.

Website:www.petsnails.co.uk/care/feeding.html

- Information on keeping snails

Website: www.bbc.co.uk/nature/species/Polar_bear#p0036tz2

- Polar bears – video footage of cubs emerging for the first time.

Website: www.spri.cam.ac.uk/resources/

- Information and resources from the Scott Polar Research Institute, including photographs.

Website:www.spri.cam.ac.uk/resources/kids/polarbears.html

- Polar bear information for children.

Website:www.bbc.co.uk/nature/animals/wildbritain/field_guides/animal_homes.shtml

- Information about homes of common British wild animals.

Website: www.animalcorner.co.uk/

- Background information and pictures relating to all types of animals.

Website:www.rspb.org.uk/

- Information about bird reserves around the country; feeding birds; wildlife gardening; identification guides and webcam footage.

Caves

ELGs: PSED 6; KUW 3, 7, 9, 10, 11

Website:http://42explore.com/caves.htm

- Information about caves and links to other cave related websites with virtual tours, cave art, maps, cave life, cave dwellers and photographs

Useful books

Fiction

Owl Babies by Martin Waddell
(Walker Books)

Who's Who in our Street by Jan Ormerod
(Red Fox)

Wolf is Coming by Elizabeth MacDonald
(Picture Lions)

Oliver's Vegetables by Vivian French
(Hodder Children's Books)

Peter Rabbit by Beatrix Potter (Warne)

Cave Baby and the Mammoth by Vivian
French (Evans Brothers)

Sleep Tight, Little Bear by Martin Waddell
(Walker Books)

The Secret Cave by Richard Hamillton
(Orchard)

Don't Wake Up the Bear! By Marjorie
Dennis Murray (Benchmark Books)

The Great Pet Sale by Mick Inkpen
(Hodder Children's Books)

Non-fiction

Caves and Crevices by Sharon Katz Cooper
(Raintree)

Home (Around the World series) by Kate
Petty (Oxfam)

Building a House by JoAnn Early Macken
(Pebble Books)

Flip Flap Farm by Katie Daynes (Usborne)

Zoo Animals 1, 2, 3 by Rebecca Fjelland
Davis (Pebble Books)

Bugs and Insects by Anthony Wootton
(Usborne Spotter's Guide)

RSPB My First Book of Garden Birds by
Mike Unwin and Sarah Whittley
(A & C Black)

RSPB My First Book of Garden Bugs by
Mike Unwin (A & C Black)

Animals in Winter by Henrietta Bancroft
and Richard G Van Gelder (Collins)

Hibernation by Anita Ganeri (Heinemann)

Gingerbread

Ingredients

- 250g margarine or butter
- 200g dark brown sugar
- 7tbsp golden syrup
- 600g plain flour
- 2tsp bicarbonate of soda
- 4tsp ground ginger.

What you do

- Heat the oven to 180°C or Gas Mark 4.

- Melt the butter, sugar and syrup in a pan.

- Mix the flour, bicarbonate of soda and ground ginger into a large bowl, then stir in the butter mixture to make a stiff dough. If it won't quite come together, add a little water.

- Roll out, on baking paper, to around the thickness of two £1 coins.

- Cut out the gingerbread shapes.

- Bake for 12 minutes or until firm.

- Leave to cool completely before decorating.

Origami house

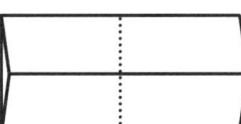

What you do

- Fold paper in half, top to bottom.

- Open up to make a centre crease.

- Fold the top and bottom halves up to meet the crease.

- Fold the paper in half widthways, make a crease and unfold.

- Turn the paper over.

- Fold right and left halves to meet the centre crease.

- Slide finger into the corner of the top 'pocket' of right side and open it up then press down to squash the pocket into a triangle shape

- Repeat with the left side.

- Turn over and draw on the windows and door.

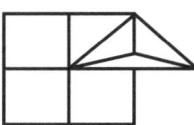

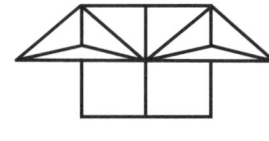

And another idea

You can use square or rectangular paper to vary the shape of the house. By changing the orientation of a rectangular sheet different sized houses can be made.

Garden creatures

ant

bee

spider

woodlouse

slug

beetle

Cheese scones

Ingredients

- 200g self-raising flour
- 50g butter or margarine
- 50g grated cheddar cheese
- 100ml milk

What you do

- Heat the oven to 200°C, Gas Mark 6.

- Cut the butter into small pieces and stir into the flour.

- Rub the butter into the flour using fingertips until the mixture looks like breadcrumbs.

- Stir in the cheese.

- Add the milk and mix with a knife or fingers until the mixture makes a soft, but not sticky dough.

- Make a ball and place on to a floured surface.

- Roll out the dough until about 2cm thick then use a cutter to cut out scone shapes.

- Place the scones on a baking sheet.

- Bake for 10 to 15 minutes until golden brown.

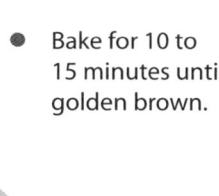

Tangram egg

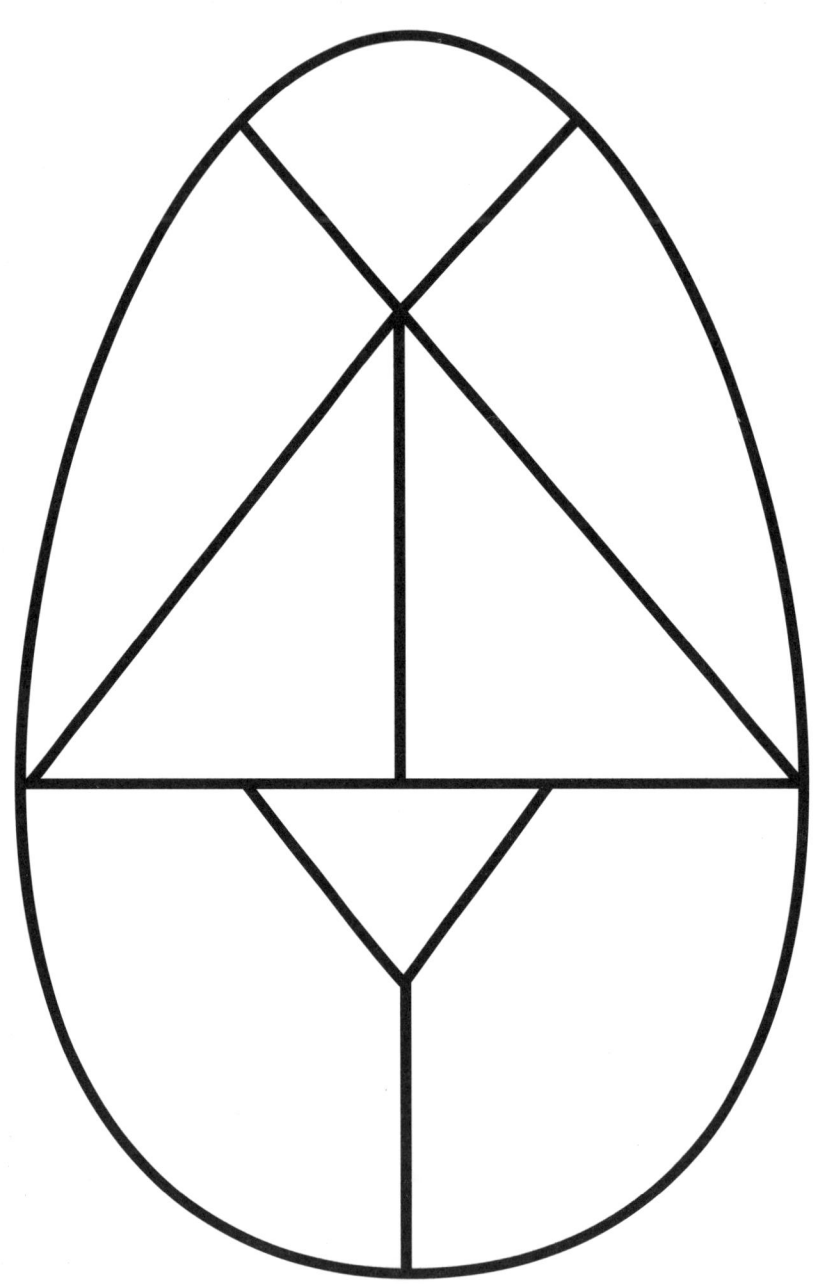